Walk Around

A City

Peter and Connie Roop

Editorial Offices: Glenview, Illinois • Parsippany, New Jersey • New York, New York
Sales Offices: Needham, Massachusetts • Duluth, Georgia • Glenview, Illinois • Coppell, Texas
• Sacramento, California • Mesa, Arizona

Big Book version of *A City* published by Scott Foresman.

ISBN: 0-328-16879-3

1 2 3 4 5 6 7 8 9 10 VO08 12 11 10 09 08 07 06 05

Contents

What Is a City?

Seattle, Washington

Salt Lake City, Utah

A city is a large **community** in which many thousands, even millions, of people live. More than half of all Americans live in cities. Cities in the United States are all different, but they are alike in some ways.

Chicago, Illinois

Boston,
Massachusetts

Austin, Texas

Atlanta, Georgia

Mapping the City

Cities have a **downtown** area. The downtown has office buildings, stores, **public transportation** stations, parks, hotels, and a **city hall**. Outside the downtown, there are homes, businesses, and factories. Buildings here aren't as tall as they are downtown.

This map shows Chicago, Illinois, the city you are walking around in this book. Chicago is the center of a large **metropolitan area**.

Chicago

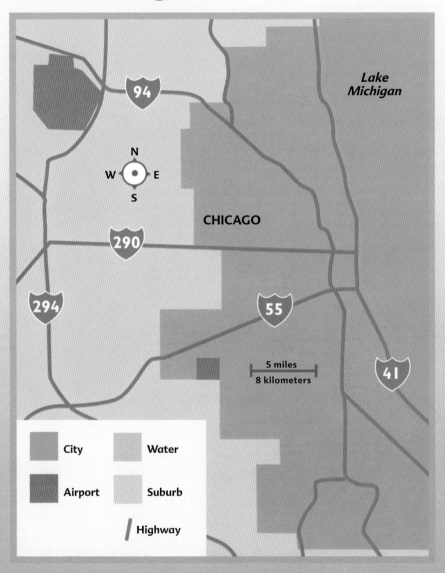

Lake Michigan

N
W E
S

CHICAGO

5 miles
8 kilometers

City   Water

Airport   Suburb

Highway

Homes

Most homes outside **downtown** are apartments, small houses, or **town houses**. Cities are divided into **neighborhoods**. Each neighborhood is different and special.

Most people downtown live in **high-rises** or apartment buildings. High-rises can tower 50 stories or more.

Getting Around

Many people do not own cars because they use **public transportation** or they walk to wherever they are going. City streets are busy during the day.

Many people in the **metropolitan area commute** to work into the city on trains or **subways**. People use public transportation to get into the city for special events or to shop.

Schools

A city has many schools and thousands of students. Many children ride to school in school buses, cars, **subways**, city buses, or even taxis.

Some city schools are very tall. This school is near **high-rises** and small shops. No matter where schools are or how big they are, they all have playgrounds.

The Police

There are many police stations in a city. There is one large station that is the **headquarters**. Each station has many police officers.

Most police officers **patrol** the city in cars. Others walk a **beat**. This helps officers to know the people in the **community**. Some officers ride horses in special areas of the city or during special events.

Working

In the **downtown** area, people work in **skyscrapers**, large office buildings, stores, restaurants, schools, and factories. Many people who live in towns and **suburbs** also come to work in the city.

Many people work in construction jobs. These people build the roads, buildings, and homes that the millions of people in a large city need.

Shopping

Many city stores are small and serve the people in nearby **neighborhoods**. These stores open early in the morning and stay open late at night.

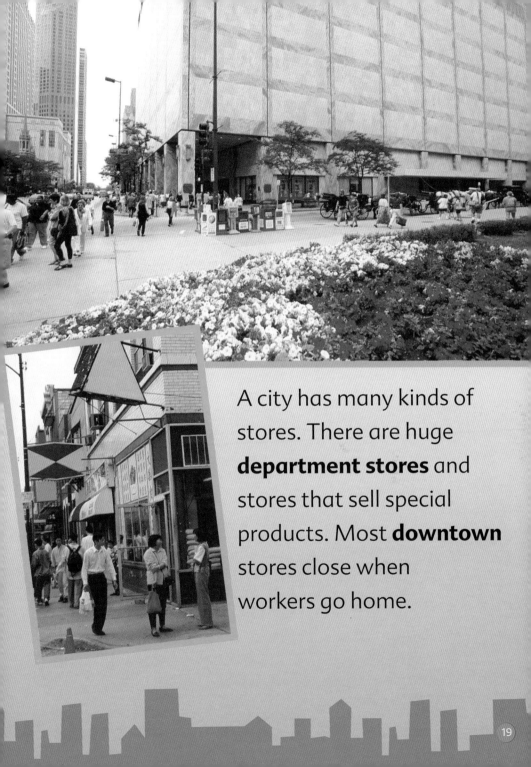

A city has many kinds of stores. There are huge **department stores** and stores that sell special products. Most **downtown** stores close when workers go home.

The Library

A big city has a main library where people borrow books and look for information. The main library is also a place where people can listen to music, see art shows, join book clubs, and see other special events.

There are many **branch** libraries in different **neighborhoods** throughout the city. People use branch libraries because they are closer to where they live.

Banks and Money

Neighborhood banks are usually **branches** of bigger banks. Most people drive to these banks. The banks have drive-up or walk-up windows.

Usually, a bank's main office is **downtown**. The main bank has many workers. Besides workers who help people with their money, the bank managers who run the bank also work there.

The Post Office

A large, main post office is usually **downtown**. Most of the city's mail goes there before being delivered.

There are also
many **branch** post
offices throughout the city. Letter carriers
walk or drive cars or trucks to deliver the
mail. In big apartment buildings, people
must go to special mailboxes to get their
mail.

Playing

Downtown and in **neighborhoods** there are parks in which to play. Many neighborhoods have block parties, festivals, or other special events.

Cities have theaters
where plays and
shows can be seen.
Many big cities also have
professional sports teams to watch. There
are art and science museums to explore and
aquariums and zoos to visit.

Helping Out

A big city is made up of many **neighborhoods,** each with many people. Together, they make up the city **community.** Many people work together to plan neighborhood events like fairs or contests.

These events raise money for special projects or to help people with special needs. By helping in their neighborhoods, people help the entire city. This makes the city a better place in which to live.

Glossary

aquariums places with fish and underwater animals

beat area police officers walk

branch smaller part of something bigger

city hall building where a city's leaders meet

community area where people live, work, and shop

commute to travel from home to work and back

department stores large stores that sell many different things

downtown area where most businesses are

headquarters place where city or business leaders work

high-rises very tall apartment buildings

metropolitan area area that includes a large city and its surrounding suburbs

neighborhood small area of a city or town where homes, streets, and other things are alike

patrol to guard or watch an area

professional sports sports in which players get paid to play

public transportation ways of travel that are organized and that everyone can use

skyscrapers very tall office buildings

suburbs towns near large cities where people live

subways trains that can run underground

town houses many homes connected together

More Books to Read

Brown, Craig. *City Sounds*. New York: Greenwillow Books, 1992.

Fallow, Allan, ed. *Do Skyscrapers Touch the Sky?* New York: Time-Life Books, 1994.

Grimes, Nikki. *C is for City*. New York: Lothrop, Lee & Shepard, 1995.

Llewellyn, Claire. *Cities*. Des Plaines, Ill: Heinemann Library, 1997.

Index